About the Author

Gill Barr was born in Londonderry
Derry Primary and Foyle and Lond
from Loughborough University, whe.
Universities. She taught English at comprehensive school
Cambridgeshire and Dorset for over thirty years. She holds an MA
in Creative Writing from Queen's University, Belfast and has
received an award for her poetry from the Northern Ireland Arts
Council.

Gill's poems have appeared in publications such as: *The Honest
Ulsterman*, *New Humanist*, *The New European*, *Bad Lilies*, *Trasna*
and *Riptide's Climate Change Matters Anthology*. Her debut
pamphlet *The Price of Violence*, included in this collection, was
Highly Commended in the 2023 Mslexia Competition. Gill read her
pamphlet at *Worlds Apart*, the inaugural event at the New Gate Arts
and Culture Centre in Londonderry in 2024.

Gill has performed at the Bridport Literary Festival, reading her
prize-winning short story *Skylight* in 2016 and her poems in 2018
alongside Annie Freud and Elaine Beckett. She appeared at the
Exeter Literary Festival in 2019 and 2021, and at the Ledbury
Poetry Festival in 2022 in a quartet with Greta Stoddart, Elaine
Beckett and Helen Evans.

Gill lives in a state of flux between Dorset and Derry/Londonderry.

Contents

A Wide River Divides Us

Gill Barr

LEAF BY LEAF

Published by Cinnamon Press
www.cinnamonpress.com

Designed and typeset in Bodini by Cinnamon Press. Cover design by Adam Craig with original artwork by Patryk Sadowski, 'Peace DNA' © Patryk Sadowski.

Cinnamon Press is represented by Inpress.

For Emma and George

A Wide River Divides Us

City Café, 1968

I climb onto a chair
in a long, low room,

see the white cloth, silver, glass,
all set for the reception,

when something that I can't see
enters the room,

something that runs
like a spooked horse among us.

It careers through the grown-ups
in their wedding

best, rushes the tables,
scattering chairs.

It gallops towards me,
leaps

inside me – never
leaves.

Gap

It's an ordinary school morning
sleepy cold and grey.

Something's happening
in the front bedroom,

Daddy is saying over and over,
It's gone!

I go in. He's at the window,
turns to Mammy, as if she hasn't heard.

She's out of bed. *You'll lose your job,* she says.
It's not the first.

They pull their clothes on,
hurry down.

I dare myself to the window,
juke round the blind,

see in our tight terraced street
the gap

a bit outside our house, a bit
outside Kearney's.

I already know what's happened and why
to us.

Soldier Doll

There's a rope round a lamppost in Ferguson's Lane
where the big girls swing.

I want to swing on the knotty twine round the blue-green post,
but don't.

To another lamppost, not far from here, a girl's been tied,
her head shaved.

She's been tarred and feathered for loving a Brit.
Soldier Lover. Soldier Doll.

Some nights I dream of her, tied up and terrified,
shamed in the street.

Great-aunt Maggie

November 1971

She was the oldest but never married
because of a bad foot kept in a boot
that came up to her knee,
laced tight
through thirty pairs of eyelets.

Her life was lived off the Dark Lane
near the gasworks with a view of the cemetery.
She walked heavily to school, church,
the shirt factory, shops,
until it was too dangerous to stay,

so with her brother and his young family,
they ceded the only home
they'd ever known,
with its built-on bathroom
and two bedrooms that once slept nine.

She died soon after of 'natural' causes,
the family's grief increased
by the fear
she might not be laid to rest
by her father and mother,

because of the armed roadblock
at the graveyard gate,
so her family stepped up to the barricades,
asked those ruling the streets
to let the hearse that was bearing her body in.

I didn't go to the funeral,
children didn't.
Hardly any men
wanted to stand out on the hill
that November day.

The women prepared a good spread
for those coming back,
after the cold stand at the exposed plot.
I remember black ties, overcoats
and barely buttoned-up rage.

Bloody Monday

31st January 1972

Here we are
at the dead end of the street,
playing three-goals-and-you're-in against Hutchie's wall,

except we're not,
because they're sitting on the kerb
looking down and away,

not up at me
with the ball at my feet
raring to play,

but they don't want to,
because yesterday
happened.

A New Cousin

February 1972

On Saturday morning
I'm allowed to see him
at Granny's, where he lives.

He's blond, wears only a nappy,
because my auntie says
the nurse is calling.

I'm shocked to see
his raised belly-button,
topped with hardened blood.

I get to hold him.
Bread-warm and wriggly,
he makes us laugh. There's news.

They are leaving Granny's
big house to get their own place
for, as my uncle says,

with the rioting, the oil-drums
set on fire and rolled down the street,
this is no place to bring up a child.

Next-door Neighbours

1ˢᵗ March 1972

The Kearneys' house is like our house, only back to front.
They have a sorrowful Jesus on the wall above a red light.

After I have my tonsils out, Mr Kearney brings me home
in a Morris Mini-van in everglade green.

Another time Mrs Kearney takes us in, because Daddy's
fallen from a ladder and Mammy's taken him for help.

When Mrs Kearney's baby's due, Daddy drives her
to hospital, telling soldiers at the check-point

to let him through or *they*'ll be doing the delivery.
One day after school we're in Woolworth's.

There's a bomb-scare. We're ushered to the cordon
at Ferryquay Gate with everyone else, chatting,

joking, juking round the ones in front to see
the action, or no action, most likely it's a hoax –

                                        Blast. Fast-slow
                                        shatter, shudder
                                        of rubble. Screams.

Mammy panics us down Carlisle Road
and home. We hear that Mr Kearney's hurt.
A piece of shrapnel hit his head.

He is away a long time.
One day we see him at the door. There's a dent
in his head. He does not speak the way he did.

Some days the words don't come to him at all
and he looks at Mrs Kearney,
as if she has them.

Claudy

31ˢᵗ July 1972

Daddy used to call at that shop
to take a biscuit order and when
he finishes telling Mammy this,

there's a darker hush than usual,
a depth of stun, of helplessness
they can't go on from.

She asks who would do this,
who would be so bad
as to kill ordinary people

going for a paper,
delivering milk. He is vexed
about the girl, my age,

who was wiping the shop-window
when the first went off,
the first of three without warning

in the same wee village
we drive through on the way
to our auntie's farm in Cookstown.

August Fortnight

There's a big grey suitcase on Mammy's bed,
another that's battered brown. We're taking
all we can because, as Mammy says,
there might not be a house to come home to.

Daddy drives us to Portrush.
We play *Who can see the sea first?*
We race to the beach, build sandcastles, ride a donkey,
get Granny a bucket of salty water for her legs.

We buy an ice-cream without getting lost,
go to Barry's, all clanging lights
and flashing din. We do the dodgems,
the helter-skelter, get breathless on the cyclone.

Granny takes us to the cinema.
We enjoy the dark.
Eat sweets.
Somebody shouts *Bomb!*

We rise and run – I put my hands out – push
into the back of the boy in front – tumble
forward in the black stampede
down the central aisle – look back for my granny

but we are being stopped – are being shooed back
to our seats. A hoax. It was just some lig,
some stupid eejit pulling our legs,
playing a sick joke.

Afloat

Car-door opening,
scrambling over bare legs to get out first,
needing the beach, being held back
to carry a deckchair,
to walk with the family
till the rug is laid down:

No, not there, further on, a bit more,
yes, there you are – Get Granny her deckchair –
Help with the windbreak – Don't step on the rug –

Now wrench off your sandals and run
like the wind into the wind,
free,
towards the high beach.

Wade the fine deep sand of the dunes,
avoid the spiky pointy grasses.
Run up the dunes and jump down.
Run up the dunes and jump down.
Run up and *throw* yourself down,
grasping the sand in your hands.
Watch it flow from your fingers.
You are happy, you are happy as never.
The wind in your ears making you
an island,
alone,
alive in the wind,
on the sand, on the move.

You race back to the red tartan rug,
breeze off your clothes to blustery wind-talk
and warnings in the ear of:
Don't go far out.

You are eager and ready and running,
alert to broke shells that might slice your sole,
hurrying over the corrugated foreshore,
a cattle-grid runner on your way to the water,
evading the wormcasts and the corpses of crabs,
skipping over the frilly pretty wavelets,
the chilly choppy wavelets, the penny-dainty splashes. Cold

dashes your knees as the water gets deeper. Cold
hits you higher so you go slower. Cold
on your thighs – then a belly-high chill
from an unbreaking wave – a slap
to your belly from a fast-breaking wave,
which you turn away from,
see the beach-squat of orangey windbreaks,
which is yours, which is –
big bare backslap returns you
to facing the water – it is coming, o it's coming,
the big one –

takes you over, takes you under,
gasping, grasping, footless, afraid,
water up your nose, alarm in the brain,
feet become pistons pounding the water,

until grateful and gasping,
you pop into air
on the flat of your back to the vast of the sky
and stretch out your surfacing,
suffering arms.

Isolated Shooting Incident

I walk home from school,
down the safe side of
Bishop Street, swinging
my new brown case.
Two Red Caps appear,
saying *Hi* in accents
from the television.
I say *Hello*, burning
red and shy. They ask
friendly questions but
I don't know how to be
like the ones who know
what to say. I can't speed
up to get away. Can't
slow down. They chat on
till we reach the old jail
that's being knocked
down, when at the corner
to Upper Bennett Street
there are shots – deafening,
epileptic shots – the Red
Caps explode, like runners
to a starting-gun, tear off
their caps, hurtle full pelt
away. I stand, then run
for Mrs Gilchrist's door,
throw myself down,
hold my school-case
tight, hammer the door.
She doesn't answer.
Then she does.
What's wrong?
I look up: *Shootin'!*
She looks round as
if she doesn't believe
me, but other women
appear, so she does.
Talk is going on
at headscarf level.
One woman says,
I'll leave her home.

She walks me down
Bennett Street, along
Maureen Avenue,
Ewing Street, Miller
Street, into our street.
She tells Mammy what's
gone on. Soon a crowd
is at our door. Mammy's
upset. I can't tell if I've
done something right
or something wrong,
so I slip away, get out
my bike, sit on it, up
the street, watch them
talk, until Mrs Kilgore
with the big mole on
her chin comes up, takes
hold of the handlebars,
stares at me through her
milk-bottle glasses, says
that what's happened
is not important,
that I will soon
forget.

The Price of Violence

Tuesday Documentary, BBC1 9.25 pm, 14th November 1972

They've come to our school. I've been chosen
to speak to them, not sure why, but Mammy knows,
so I've had to wear a lilac dress, when I prefer trousers
for football with the boys at breaktime.

I'm collected from my classroom, walked through
the Headmaster's room to what we call the TV Room.
Today our TV has been shut away. Giant lights,
huge loops of wire and seats are there instead.

A man in a suit invites me to sit. He's kind.
We chat. He gives me two wine-gums.
After a few weeks comes the broadcast
our house has been dying for.

I see myself on screen – bolt to the kitchen,
hide behind the red ironing-board,
next to the coal bucket by the backdoor.
It goes quiet. I dare to juke in, hear myself speak

about playing *Spotlight* in the street, how I spot
somebody hiding in our passage, sneak up with the torch,
turn it on, full beam, in his face, saying, *Caught ye*,
see the big eyes of a blacked-up soldier, pointing a gun.

What did you do then? asks the presenter.
                    I nearly died.
The room erupts because I am very Derry
– it's back to the ironing-board for me.

When I come out, it seems I've done alright.
Valerie has called from the phone-box at Tillie's Brae
and Alec Connor, from across the street, has left
a shiny 50p for me on the sideboard.

Night Terrors

There's something moving under my bed,
something alive. I must get to the door,
put foot to floor – feel a hairy body
against me, see disappear onto the landing
our black dog, Dougal, who never
comes up the stairs on Mammy's orders,
but for reasons best known to himself,
he has made the forbidden journey.
I will not tell on him, but will remember
the fear, like the night I heard tap, tapping,
at my window, pulled the curtain
I-can-reach-from-my-bed back,
saw a gunman – it must have been
a gunman – out on the roof.
I don't tell because it's my terror,
due to all the trouble in the streets,
the flood of bad news, or perhaps inherited,
because when Granny stayed over
and slept in my bed with me, she woke up,
raised her head off the pillow, and called out
for George, my daddy, her son.
She called three times.
He didn't come.
I asked her what was wrong.
She whispered, *There's a person over there,
in front of the wardrobe.*
I peered into the dark. *It's ok, Granny.
It's only my pyjama case with the Aunt Sally
face, all big eyes, brash eyelashes and red wool
for hair.* Granny said, *Oh,*
and went back to sleep.

Endeavour

She has the pink hands of a florist,
cold to the touch, a shock
because the heart is warm of the ever-girl,
who knows our names, our families,
the history of us, sends us birthday cards
with a picture of our Saviour
and a text such as, 'Suffer the little children...'

which is the image I look up at every Sunday
in the stained glass gallery-window
on our side of the church,
an image in which Jesus with open hands
is mobbed by mothers holding babies
and children at his feet,
looking up.

On Mondays we have our tea
and are on time for CE, which she leads.
If we're early, we help set out the round
of honey-varnished chairs and a table
at the front on which she puts the roll-book
and the cream tin with blue flowers on it
that holds the sweets for later.

There are Bible stories, characters we know
by their first names, Peter, Moses, Ruth,
like extended family. We sing choruses
with actions, stretch our arms *Wide, wide as the ocean...*
We do a Bible search, find a verse, stand up
to read out first. I love the words,
the competition.

A navy pouch, like a pocket
without its trousers, gets passed round
for the collection, as we sing:
Dropping, dropping, dropping, dropping
    Hear the pennies fall...
Then we bow our heads in prayer.
At last, a sugary pastille from the tin.

Routine Tuesday at the Girls' Brigade

I walk to the church hall in my uniform,
only to hear there's no getting into squads,
no marching to Scottish tunes, no drill
competition which I love and sometimes win,
no games, no running hard to the front of the hall,
throwing myself on the *Rocks*, no pelting
against the tall cupboards at the back, shut
as a *Ship's* hull, no sprawling on the *Lifeboats*
of the windowsills to watch flapping wallpaper
in a bombed-out shop. None of this.

I am to be walked out of my known
world, to a convention far away.
I don't want to take the bridge
over the dark river. Some distress
must show, because talk goes on.
A decision is being made. A big girl
will miss the convention
to walk me home. She chats us
up Abercorn Road. I feel safe
with her, a mute relief
that lasts till our doorbell.

Mammy listens to her story,
thanks her, takes me in,
says, *What's wrong with you anyway?*
not waiting for the answer,
because I have embarrassed her,
let the side down, broken the routine.

Coleraine

12th June 1973

Daddy is home from work.
Something very bad
has happened. A bomb.
Coleraine. It was close.
People are dead. The blast
blew Daddy's car around
the corner. The rear wind
-screen burst from its
fittings, ended up on
the backseat, intact.
A policeman said:
You should be dead.

Learning to Swim

We walk from our school on the city walls
to Butcher's Gate, drop down the hill
by the high-rise flats, along walkways
that seem safe on Wednesday mornings.

We see bricks, broken paving-stones, angry graffiti,
glimpse *Free Derry* wall. Some days we spot rubber-bullets
in the gutter but we have seen public information
films and know not to touch.

We walk on as if invisible,
reach the boarded-up public baths by the back door.
We learn how to breath under water,
how to dive for sunken blocks.

In the din of the pool or cut off from it,
we gain our distance badges:
ten, twenty-five, fifty, a hundred meters,
going farther and nowhere at the same time.

Saturday Night, Bath Night

We were well washed, wrapped in towels
and dried off by the fire. We put on clean
pyjamas and learned our catechism for Sunday.
One time Mammy was washing my hair
in the kitchen-sink when a bomb went off.
I banged the back of my head on the mixer-tap.

She hurried from the house. I had this feeling
in my chest like a balloon inflating. We stood
at our front-door, watching people gather in the street.
Aye, it's close that one, somebody said, and the man-
with-the-radio-that-could-intercept-the-police-frequency
said, *It's Abercorn Road.*

Mammy was on her way to 33 where her mammy lived.
She must have hurried down Miller Street, up
Ewing Street, into Maureen Avenue, not knowing
what she was going to. She must have seen
the garage behind Granny's blown sky high,
while Granny watched the TV.

She must have seen the back windows blown in:
the big window of the high kitchen, the small
square scullery-window, the frosted bathroom-window,
the bedroom windows of the tall, angular house.
Glass must have flown everywhere and where Granny
was when it flew in, I never knew.

Granny was angry at people traipsing through her home,
though they were only helping to sweep up the glass
and put up plastic-sheeting before night fell,
but she felt invaded, was livid at the damage, its cause,
when she'd kept 33 clean all her life, washed her front-step
every week, made her brasses gleam.

She was taken to my auntie's in the Waterside
and hardly returned. The big house was emptied,
her treasures dumped or stored.

Years later, my mother recalled how she and my auntie
broke ruby-glass into a bin so nothing was left behind
when the house was sold at a knockdown price
to people who would be safe living in that street.

Sharp Shooter

I love my lessons
but live for break and lunch
when we flood into the covered playground

and play. We understand where the goal is,
what is post, what's crossbar.
Even when the juniors cross to their toilets,

we keep on tackling, winning the ball back,
getting free to receive a pass or make one.
We shimmy-and-shoot towards the boy

with the gloves who dives-and-saves
or dives-and-misses or just dives,
not bothered by concrete.

On wet days the rain blows through the railings
so the playground puddles.
We play anyway.

On sunny days we play in Stable Lane
with coats for goalposts. We live
with the *for you* / *against you* effects of the slope.

The pace is furious, except at shoot-outs,
when it slows.
It's you against him.

Do you shoot with your left foot like Lorimer?
Do you place it with your right foot
like Clarke? Choose.

The thrill of victory, the agony of defeat
between the clanging
of the swung
bell.

A Dance Lesson

After school on Tuesdays our classroom becomes deranged for dancing. It seems we are to flit about, not really dancing or being taught to dance. We are just to shift our weight from foot to foot, slightly shaking our bent arms. Mrs Oliver is light on her feet, how her toes point, but I don't like her singing along to *Chirpy, Chirpy, Cheep, Cheep*.

Now we are *Riding Along On Our Pushbikes, Honey*, circling the room with high knees, as if we're cycling. Some of us slump against the wall. I lie, listening to new songs, look down at the floorboards, up at the high windows, notice the mesh that usually stops the bottles from the Bog, also bricks, and sometimes petrol bombs.

The song changes: this one is not about pushbikes or puppy love; it's about our everyday, the soldiers we see in the sentry-post at the top of the lane or at checkpoints or patrolling our streets. They used to come into the house for tea, stacking their rifles by the door like haystooks. One of them was called Chip – he had a chipped tooth. He gave us cap badges. On holiday in Portrush I spotted a picture of him in Granny's *Mirror*, visited by the Prince of Wales in a military hospital. He'd been shot. I knew him by his tooth.

In this sad song, a soldier like Chip lies down on a bomb. To save others. I listen to every word, hear what he's thinking as he waits to die... anguished, in tears...

The big girls are pulling me to my feet, a bouncy pop tune comes on. I must join in. Mrs Oliver watches. I must jig up and down. I must go round and round. I must not be so sensitive, so serious, so myself.

Cul-de-sac

My daddy arrives home, shouting,
*Help me empty the car – they're
comin' for it!* No time to ask.
We're carrying boxes into the house,
when two men appear. One pulls a gun
on Daddy, says, *Giv' us yer keys.*
You're not gettin' them, he replies.
Giv'us yer keys, repeats the gunman.
I'm watching my daddy at gunpoint,
my daddy resisting this outrage.
Giv'us yer keys! shouts the gunman.
Daddy knows himself defeated, says:
*If ye want them, ye can bloody go
and get them.* He hurls the keys
across the street. The sidekick
is bolting, is plucking the keys
from the gutter, sprints to the car,
starts it, throws it roughly forward
and back, till it's facing out of the street.
The gunman jumps in beside him.
They speed away. Nobody moves,
until Mammy darts to the phone,
picks up the receiver, dials, gets
an answer – from the Bogside Inn!
She shouts, *Tae Hell's gates wi' ye!*
slams the phone down, tries again,
gets through: *But what can we do?*
she sobs, *Nothin'. Nothin'.*
The police won't come.
Later, Daddy says his house-key
is with his car-key. Our home
isn't safe. He will head over the bridge
to his locksmith friend, taking Mammy
for the walk, to steady her nerves,
so me and my brother are to stay
and our uncle will be down soon
to look after us, so we wait
in the living-room by the goldfish
on the sideboard. They swim
in the murky bowl, nuzzle a dark
plant. A flake of food floats – a knock
on the door. We look at each other.

What should we do? We move together
into the hall, towards the front-door.
We call out: *Who's there?*
The letterbox opens.
A deep voice says, *A holy man.*
I burst into tears, thinking a priest
has been sent to seize us,
but my brother says it's only our uncle
being stupid, so he undoes the snib
and lets him in. I hurry to tell him
what has happened, that two gunmen
came to our house and took our car away.

Scene Around Six

There's killing or bombing
every day. Everyone watches for
is it one of ours or one of theirs.

If it's one of ours that's bad.
if it's one of theirs,
most likely they deserved it,

though you know that's not really true
because you already see with your own eyes
there's good and bad on both sides.

When the politicians *condone the violence*
you can't tell from their faces
what that means.

Sometimes the news presenter says,
A man is helping the police with their inquiries
which sounds kind, but you soon learn it's not.

Some days the presenter's lips are extra thin.
He says, *You may find some of these scenes disturbing.*
Mammy tells you to leave.

You wait in the hall fearing how she'll be.
Will she put her hands in her hair,
squeeze it tight and say,

O for the wings of a dove
– you're afraid
she'll fly away.

Why We Leave Cook Terrace

February 1975

We're moving
to the Waterside. We're
thrilled to see our new house,
clatter up and down its stairs,
lie on the new carpet, smell the fresh
paint, enjoy the airy rooms
without furniture, eat our lunch like a picnic
off the floor, but something's not right.
Mammy is crying. She doesn't want
to move. She has lived all her life
in the same streets, no matter
she is moving to a better
house and safer.

On moving day we use a green van
not meant for removals. Mammy
holds a hankie to her face,
then sobs aloud: *We are flittin'.*
She's ashamed.
She has let the side down
after all these years, but Daddy
has been threatened in late-night
phone-calls – he has been told to get out
or face the consequences – he has been dragged
into the alley off Maureen Avenue
and told at gunpoint to get out
or be shot.

Grinning Bobby

November 1975

Once I was in the big pool with a new inflatable,
the colour of strawberry Angel Delight on one side,
whipped cream on the other.

A big boy called Bobby was splashing about.
He took my new ring without asking
and swam away.

Later when he flung it back, the steel pin
with the round head that kept the air in
had gone.

I told Daddy who sent him diving
to find it. After several tries,
he surfaced, spluttering,

handed me the pin, grinning wildly,
all pleased with himself and thrashed off
to irk someone else.

I never thought much of him,
never thought of him at all – now this:
he's been shot

ten times
in the back and in the head.
I know grinning Bobby and he's dead.

Fifty Years On

We are watching a Sunday night drama
that starts with a bombing. My father
says *That's not entertainment.*

He starts talking about Coleraine, the story I know
about his car blown round the corner, the policeman
saying *You should be dead* but he goes on,

tells how he stepped out of his car that day.
It was just like that he says nodding at the television,
the dust, the devastation. People were just lying there,

one old woman, they were collecting her up,
putting her in an ambulance. I saw her glasses
amongst the debris. I picked them up,

gave them to the policewoman.
It was just like that, the dust,
the devastation.

Keep Walking

After the hold up at the house,
I saw one of them
in Bishop Street, followed
the same boy down the Dark Lane,

then I said to myself,
What d'you think you're doing?
Catch up with him – what then?
I turned on my heel and came home.

Another time, in Maureen Avenue,
in clear daylight, they stuck a gun
in my stomach, took me into the ally,
put me up against the wall, asked for ID.

Maybe they thought I was a policeman
in plain clothes, because of my short
hair and fawn overcoat. I started
cheekin' them up a bit.

They heard the accent, started talking
between themselves, so I stepped out
into Maureen Avenue – kept walking,
waiting for a bullet in my back.

A man I knew was passing. Mr Foster,
I said, keep walking. I've just been held up.

His eyes were standing in his head,
but he stayed with me to the end of the street,
then he turned right to his house
and I went left to mine.

Privilege

Well, they had wealth, they had power
they wanted to keep it to themselves
and people like us, well, you were basically

told who to vote for, but I was lucky
because I was brought up in a mixed area
Catholics and Protestants together

and the house I bought with your mother
was in a mixed street
and I never had problems with anyone.

We were all working people
and we all had the same problem,
barely enough money...

***

The Road to Shroove

A passing van says *Make Me Up*
but I couldn't if I tried

or perhaps I'm already in on the act
of imagination before I know it.

Might I be made up from the dimpling
of that one cloud in all the blue

from the fortitude of the lighthouse
and the wonky sequencing of telegraph-posts?

Am I made up from that line of long light
on the opposite shore

from a sort of silvered belonging stretched out
near any horizon?

Don't mention the memory of the fury of the sea
against the black rocks, says she.

Remember the allure of the rose-hips
and berries on the mountain ash, says he.

I am what this place has made me,
a bag of assorted items for the nature table,

an accumulation of voices and the art
of the troubles.

There is violence in the grass as well as growth.

Magilligan Point

You stand in the downpour, feet sinking into the wet sand
under the stubbed gaze of the Martello tower.

Scallops, mussels and razor clams lie strewn around you
like casualties of the last invasion.

You are held in this cusped place of pushed
sediment and extreme water.
A little way out is instant
depth.

You stand armoured with insignificance
small with wonder,

watching for import in the turbulent clouds
and roughening sea.

Who comes to rescue or subdue?
No god, no hero appears,

only the local ferry shuttling back and forth
on its known course.

The latest squall forces you back
to the dunes,

where spiked grasses thriving on burial
brace the sand.

Lisfannon

Stripped back
to what survives
without encouragement

they work
silenced by the wind
beyond weary of the long wet.

From the land
they wrestle rock
to build homesteads

block life into low rooms
to contain their hope
keep it dry.

To hold back the hill
they build stone walls
mortared by dark.

They herd their fear
in fields angled for resistance
marked by shut gates.

Up the hard hill they well
the water that sustains them
drives them to the edge

where hope
looks like despair
and dry is mere anticipation of wet.

Some mute pleasure
reticent as berries on the rowan
is found in a sky less grey

or in cloud speed.
Toughened as broom
capable of blossom

they hold on
between the shifts of promise
and certainty of doubt

waiting
for the prodigal
sunshine and punishing rain.

They Came Out of the Mist

They came out of the mist in their log-boats, hugging the coastline,
nudging their way along river channels, into riverbanks
to find a clearing for the season,
from which to fan out on foot in search of food.

They came back, eons after, tooled up, intending to stay,
built enclosures, believing in a new way of being,
lived from a fixed point under the sky's shift and unreachable line,
realities they held first in their minds, then realised in stone, metal, bone.

Entanglements of settlement and local tensions grew.
Each tribe attuned to its own chief was harnessed to the horse
of his message. Out of each skirmish, meaning was spun,
every action woven to the single end of kin, kith, king,

until a significant arrival or re-arrival: an old boy done good
returning with a new myth and a better way
of telling it. How could they refuse
an unmatchable Saviour never before seen?

They saw he was a man on a mission
bringing a strange new force to bear on their battles, burials, brides.
He took charge of the sacred sites, enclosed them,
made the chiefs look ordinary, not kings.

How long would they stand it? Forever, it seemed
because the invisible was his domain. He had the Word,
could out-talk them, out-fox them at every turn,
until they took the right turn into the black church.

Life hummed on with the usual triumphs and tribulations,
good times requiring gratitude, bad times penance.
Serving a god they could only access through him,
the chieftains were grounded, though allowed

to ascend the high mounds for sacred rites,
but always they were mediated, kept low, their dominance
presented as a matter of God's grace, any defeat
due to some hellbent havoc they'd have to atone for.

Always the out-fox was beyond their known boundaries,
above them even, and life rattled along for centuries,
until new arrivals necessitated the unthinkable:

working together with erstwhile foes.

They could not match the wave of incomers
and had to bend the knee. No disrespectful thing of itself,
they said, declaring their moves strategic
even when pushed beyond the Pale.

The old guard hated the subjection. The young
progressives scooted off to distant domiciles,
preferring the new-fangled ways of far-off courts,
but the novelty waned, and the old grievances grew.

Failed rebellions sent the chieftains scrambling
for departing boats, bound for ever more distant backers,
as more settlers arrived with a new tick-box theology,
all clear-sighted and catechised,

fired up, expecting Eden, but found themselves harried
at every turn. They hunkered down but sensed
their tetchy destiny:
never to feel settled in their new land.

And so it went on, endless power grabs,
rapprochements, casual atrocities rewoven as heroics,
martial tales told partially and partly, politicking,
machinations as the next line of leaders

crunched over the skulls of the old,
in a fierce urgency for change,
to become the moment's master, allied to big ideas,
sometimes with boundaries, sometimes not.

Was there a moment, settler, when you wondered
whether life was meant to be about land and possession,
about the fixing of symbols of loss in the present,
vanquished and vainglorious, killers and killed?

Was there a moment, settler, when you yearned
for a world without stricture, for life in the motion
of wind in the grass, of light on the water, streamed
wordless instants, in the full gleam, on the go?

Dunagree Point During Rain

Three blue tents
in the far corner
of the small girl's field

blether like billy-o
in a bigger-than-breeze.

Turf smokes in the nostrils
and two escaped sheep
are pursued by a rusty boy

with a face like fuchsia
shouting *Opan tha git – quick!*

The upright lighthouse
in black and white
is edgy

as a fifty pence piece
pervious to slow time.

Into the squall
that vanishes Benevenagh
across the lough

shags hurry
and orange buoys bob.

All this, plus the rain
peppering my hood like gunfire,
so my chin deep buried in the collar of my coat

angles my gaze to a fern's wet handprint
and the happiness of harebells.

Beyond the hedgerow
I imagine the narrow strait
where open yawls

once left the lough to haul in terrors
the stifled water rushing wide

and down
into the deep attic
of the dark Atlantic.

Port-na-Garley

A solitary heron
lands on the barnacled rocks
at Port-na-Garley.

I watch him shake his head,
step with the poise of a long-limbed fop
onto a blackened rock.

He steps again where sea-pinks
sprout on the outcrop – strikes a pose.
With a flick of his doublet sleeves

he scarce takes off before he lands
on an island rock, becomes
a study of thought in grey.

I need him to carry feelings
from me – when he collapses
all conscious verticals, planes away over the airy lough,

all winged power and horizontals,
flying his cargo of languid ease
and my freight of living with aloneness.

Tremone

The least alone I've ever been
was standing once with you at Tremone
a day of sun in our bones

and no open future.
Your arm shawled me,
my arm brooch-clasped your waist.

We stood between rocks,
watching waves of schist pause,
then split,

waves in which an hour before I'd tumbled
and was borne in fearful, exhilarate alone,
while you stood watching.

Morning Recreation on the Wee White Strand

A still morning after a night of rain
and everything has its beauty

even the flung seaweed
from which she picks wrinkled sea-belt, sea-lettuce,

bladder wrack and dabber lock, the reds
of coralline and carrageen,

immersed in re-creation
she will soon call me to see.

The rock behind her
rests

like a wreck upon the sand,
its hull

a memory of presence between prow
and stern, worn still

by water
that mauvely laps,

rippling the translation
of rock and sky.

Votive

It was hours and a seashore away
that I dreamed along the water's edge
of Mac Lir's golden boat.

She combed the foreshore, picking up
driftwood with the face of an owl,
a whelk silvered, an auger barnacled

like an ice cream cone, conjoined
shells delicate and pink as babies' nails.
She straightened suddenly, walked to me,

as if about to impart the deepest secret
of the son of the sea, as if bringing
blue cauldrons of plenty.

A Drop of the Black Stuff and Some Sparkling Water

That night in August I had one too many,
so after I finally fell asleep, I woke up
to the in-breath of a snore
that turned the boiler on at four forty-nine
and startled me into sitting up
in my eighteen-inch-wide bunk,
alarmed at the job interview
I'd been undergoing in my sleep
– relieved to escape but gutted
not to know whether I got the job –
sore too because the roof of my mouth
was raw from scalding coffee I'd drunk
in Maud's of Moville that afternoon,
which meant my focus was on the pain,
when I drove by the cruise ship anchored off Greencastle,
a cruise ship so colossal you couldn't miss it.
But I did. Once it was pointed out, I saw it
loom over the warehouses of Foyle Fisheries,
saw a trail of pumpkin coaches
from which ageing tourists spilled
and just then for some reason I understood
that daughters become their mothers,
otherwise the day passed off without incident,
except it didn't because I turned unwontedly to drink
– an overstatement, it not being shy of thirty years
since last I felt a room spin, an experience
which is not quite the same as feeling the earth move.
Anyway, I sat up and reached for sparkling water
which hissed and sprayed as I undid the lid.
A glug or two later, I slunk out under
cover of drunkenness and found myself
under such a spattering of stars,
that my already sinking self-esteem
plummeted like the meteor
that hit the Irish heartland in twenty fourteen.
By the slipway I was sober,
chose a sensible rock and sat cross-legged,
looking up in daft wonder at the effervescing night-sky,
undetected by all the sleepers on narrow berths in static caravans.

Three Pints Along the Inishowen 100

The first was at Simpson's in Carndonagh
because one of our party was busting for the loo
and it seemed a plan while waiting for him
to have a sup of the black stuff, iron-smooth,
frothy rings slinking down the glass, *glas*
which I learn from the beermat means 'green',
so placenames I've always wondered at,
like Money*glass*, make total sense,
which is more than can be said
for my blethering under the influence
but it is the holidays and I'm not driving.
All the same, I've noticed the poster
in the Ladies that says, *Crashes take lives*,
and around a large photo of a child
with a ninety-nine are small photos
of those affected by his death,
which turns me to thinking how true that is,
the rippling effects of grief...

The second was at Ballyliffin Golf Club,
because our destination restaurant closed early
and some of our party needed help getting over
the disappointment of not sampling Nancy's
world championship-winning chowder,
so we went to the golf club and took a table
with a view of the mountains, the course
and the sea. If anything would make you
want to play golf, it is sitting with a drink
on a sunny afternoon, looking out over the *glas* course.
Conversely, if anything would make you
not want to play golf, it is sitting with a drink
on a sunny afternoon, overlooking the *glas* course
because the ambiance evokes the well-to-do,
like Durcan's mum. In fact, if you want to see
social exclusion writ large, visit a golf club.
If ever you are mad enough to create a society
of equals, begin by re-writing the rules
of golf clubs, though you must accept
some members will have the spondulicks
to create a new version of the old thing,

thereby keeping their exclusivity intact.
Did I say that out loud?
I did. Better keep on
sipping the Guinness and looking out
the window and soon I'm enjoying
the alcohol-ed ineffable of the majestic, freckled
hills, the sweeping *glas* of the fairways,
the driving Atlantic *gorm* of sea
and sky, letting the laughter and chatter
drown out the still, small voice...

The third was at Rosato's
where a man with *glas*
eyes was propping up the bar.
He had a face I knew or one
that stood for many. Somebody
leaned in and told me his name.
I remembered, like a shot,
how once I looked over
his mother's house with a view
to buying it – or, more exactly, with a view
to buying the view; and when the mother's name
turned out to be the same as my own, well,
it was like a sign from above, especially
as there was a five-litre holy-water container
half-full on the windowsill,
but it came to nothing.
Seamus the Bread came up, asked
if I was somebody's daughter and, indeed, I am
somebody's daughter but not the somebody
whose daughter he thinks I am.
I make for the Ladies.
A woman smiles. I smile back.
When I return, she's talking to my friends.
Now she's staring into my face.
We know we are wearing ourselves
like disguise. We see inside our ageing
to the girls we once were. She
is without doubt the one who was
the epitome of poise at school:
intelligent, lovely, good at everything.
She hugs me warmly. Old shyness
rushes in like the tide. No matter,

there are plenty here to stoke the chat,
while I rally and remember her granny,
who lived in our street and sat out
on nice days on her high step
with boiled sweets for us wee ones,
which is how I came to inherit
this girl's school uniform and books.
I could write a book about our street,
how it got lost and why, but that's a story
for another day. The waiter is reciting
the specials and after so much
of the *dubh* stuff
there's a danger of the maudlin,
which in the interests of joviality,
is best suppressed.

A Wide River Divides Us

A pied wagtail skitters across the parade ground,
as girls cut the corner to the Peace Bridge,
take a selfie with the hills and the wide river,
which is lilac in the blinking of their eyes
and has a sheen, a semi solidity, until cut
open by one jet ski on patrol. Water
arcs left and right, so two wakes
signal across the dark
water, disturb the unconscious,
slap both embankments.

People are walking, stopping for talking: on bicycles,
tricycles and scooters; they're on mobiles; hatted,
coated and booted; dogs are pulling
on leashes; cars run parallel
to the Guildhall; and I'm part of the great curve
reaching a new view of the widening bay
that narrows at Culmore,
opens out, narrows again, where pre-Christians
worshipped the sun's arrival
in the gap

between two shores, a world of twins,
like those in a stroller
in matching fleeces, one calm,
the other screeching at all these people walking,
all this water running, all this light flooding the river
and failing. The KFC car park is packed
with seagulls, the bronze family by Sainsbury's
looks forward and back. A train clacks past
the safe houses of friends, along the bay
below the new hillside cemetery, where my mother lies.

I turn from the quay and sweep through streets
of gone grandeur, past former
flashpoints, skirt round the walled city,
arrive in old haunts,
feeling out of place or disguised.
In Bishop Street I cross on a red light,
head towards Upper Bennett Street,
when a woman appears,
asks if she can reach the bridge
that way.

Local again, I nod.
She hurries off but I want to stop her,
tell her that I was born and raised here,
my mother, my grandmother too,
that we had to leave, that thousands left.
I want to tell her about this corner,
what happened,
over fifty years ago,
surprised at the swell of memory,
the force of belonging.

Suddenly weary, I aim for Bishop's Gate
and my old school on the walls,
now a centre for Verbal Arts,
rest on the Double Bastion,
our old playground,
look out over the Bogside
to *a green hill far away* that's no longer so green,
to the old hillside cemetery
where my ancestors lie
and I rarely go.

Big murals
stare up from the Bog
at the mute stub of the past
and I wonder where I go from here,
by which bridge I should re-cross the river
to get back home.

Palmer's Moon

The trees drip with dropped rain.
Mist too numb to rise rests on the ripening dark.

Day birds have all but stilled when an owl shifts
in the valley and I become aware

through October's overshot hedgerow
of a sudden light on the ridge top.

I seek a gateway, see from behind the ridge crest
and through the beech-line, a vast moon rising,

hazed in orange, formal, buoyant, full.
At a moment when I might sink

between griefs marked in time,
here is a light, visionary or mere whimsy,

surrogate for the banished mother and the vanished boy,
unstopping companion for the figure at the gate,

who walks on between the hedgerows
of black-berried night to the village,

where dark trees and shady thatches tower,
under a damson sky.

Paint for me, Mr Palmer, worlds beyond
the ordinary and within,

Frame the moon traversing this evening, you
who know better than I, the secret of the moon's saving,

its languid pull over the moil of a chalk valley
in a dreamy nocturne of bewitched belonging.

Harbour Afternoon Before the Clocks Go Back

I can't see for glare,
hear a squeaking
bike

become a pair of slanting scissors
cutting across the concrete
darkly.

Chill catches the ears,
as an engine churns and I hope
for something that eludes me,

single
on this seat looking forward
to sitting on a seat looking forward.

A gull cries out from its bastion,
as a car reversing down
the slipway

backs a trailer into the water
for the winter
haul out.

I remember Airfix models, stories
of grey ships scuttled in the collective
memory or lodged

in the graveyard at the back of the mind
of the old fella on a stick
who watched his ship go down

and returned home dumb with terror,
four hours in Atlantic waters
before rescue,

his slow shuffle from a blasted hip
no cover or good cover for fear,
unshared.

They wonder why he's like he is.
He wonders why he held on and where
it's leading,

how at certain times you doubt
the givens of your tribe,
suspect the leaders

and their acolytes,
doubt their competence,
question their adherence to the latest new,

so tiresome
as one wave reaches the inevitable
and another builds.

O man, o woman,
how we delude ourselves
with novelties,

technologies, love
of country or group
or good.

If the old fella looked me in the eyes,
I would drop them,
I would scrap this poem too.

I'd rather he knows I know it's futile
than that he thinks I'm gemmed
in some deceptive pleasance, when I'm not.

I will write until I stop, knowing
in the end it makes no odds to me
and fewer odds to others,

because at the time of passing the luff,
I won't be thinking about poetry
and others won't be asking.

Waiting becomes jading,
keeping an eye out for beauty,
trying not to leave behind a mess.

O, half-moon print,
tell me how to speak of the low sun
as the fishing-boat chugs in,

for I am feeling time's threat,
while the crew,
indifferent to the seagulls,

don't see the airborne fracas
of five fighting
over a nicked fish,

which is dropped to a splash,
pulled five ways
then pinched by the victor,

the losers floating into four corners
of an empty square,
settling upon the empty surface of things.

Tie it up and call me in,
past the smokers in the shelter,
the child in the herring-bone sweater,

the bare-armed couple. A sailor
hoses the deck. The draw of the winched
catch thins out.

Shadow stretches one ship's mast
to a finger pointing
at the top of an apartment block

from where the view
maintains the everyday deceit of the sun
setting.

Night Fishing

We arrive late at the house and sleep
or try to.

Though I am finally beside you
I cannot rest

worrying about the unwelcome.

You wake
think out loud about what we need.

I cast an arm into the darkness,
snag nothing,

slip heavily into a lough of silted
forms with staring eyes,

cold caudal fins and a flick
of tail-beat.

I must break the surface
of the day,

and still dripping, follow
across a carpet,

over a floor
of stone.

Keep

Keep your shredding seaweed hope hidden in the murky depths,
rooted to the turbid rocks.

Let it twist and sway to the current's capricious ways
with a beauty weird in water,

as Ophelia's let-down hair,
fascinating from a scalp, fastened to a skull

soon to be smooth as a slipper-limpet,
picked clean by a gull.

Night Promenade

I circle the pier end
where a soft rain glitters,
alights.

From the dark beach
the squeals of the winter young
carry

and I see the cliff
recede
like a great wedge under a vast door,

holding open
memory of holiday,
fey hope or belief in the almanac,

in the coursing of damp breath
through the pulmonary dark
or sailing the night-blue of chemistry and habit.

What is a wave
but a grey cloud grounded?
What is its spill but the illusion of ending?

Now all thought is hooded,
hoicked, hung from the gibbets
of municipal lighting.

Thoughts that were golden as goblets,
jocund as chocolate,
inapt as filberts with limpets,

become a muddle of respite,
then murder,
then the music of stones

rubbing shoulders
to the grind of the water,
the tune of the sailors,

the sons and the daughters,
floating in time, in cavities,
in cells

of seconds and minutes,
closing in, closing in,
like the dark.

Line in the Sand

Leaning on a rail looking out
at the high waves rushing in, fury
in those waves – I love their force

against the rocks, their pow and plosion,
giant spray throwing its head forward
like any sea monster, shattering

into pieces and gone.
All sea-myths live in the deep
imagination. All mariners fear

the protean sea while the islanders
hug the coast, hug themselves tight
against high tides in the inlets, the rias,

the soft bays. Some resist the inevitable,
shunt the problems up the coast.
Others live with the edge,

knowing there is no division,
only words dividing one from the other;
no sea, no shore, only gradations

of life attuned to the changing.
In the mingle they all live at one
with the now of the downpour,

landslip, inundation, but in the calm
after the storm, in the dread
of the next storm, as the harbour-lights

come on, go off, as the boats go out,
come in, with a catch or no catch,
as day arrives, then night, when voices

cry out for certainty, some hoist flags,
name themselves and the other, draw a line
in the sand, control their waters,

but fish continue their indiscriminate
travels across boundaries, voyagers
take chances, viruses slip in,

unstoppable exchanges
between wave and shore, between
spray and sand.

Any developed south-easterly or easterly condition, or
a southerly gale, will cause the sea to break so heavily
at the entrance as to make the harbour unapproachable

There is no easy way to enter the harbour on a rough day.
Arrival depends upon your skill,
your craft and acceptance
of forces you cannot see
to ensure you pass safely
between the red and green
lights, surge into the relative calm
of the outer harbour where you drop sail,
activate the motor and putt, putt in so casually
your spare hand reaches for the sponge and busies itself
on the deck. You push the tiller to port, let it alone and slosh
more freely, enjoying, like a one-winged gull, the circular spool.

A thought seeps through: the riot of water and wind is passing you by,
sailors are still out there on the swell, enthralled, taut
with intent, while you idle in circles,
your land-life closing in.
You'll moor,
climb the fixed ladder
to the harbourside, make your way
through heavy traffic to the superstore for
essentials, *en route* to a crisis that was not resolved
before you left. Thoughts of true home are out there on the water,
along with the memory of a dream you had this morning, just as you woke,
of an old fisherwoman on stilts, looking down on you, saying, *Tend-er, tend-er.*

West Dorset Spring

I walk into the moment
of the pushing primroses becoming
beneath the unborn tree.
I long to weaken
against the deep green velvet
of the horseback tree
and let the wooded sky
grow over me.

Albino deer appear,
a spectral two,
who stare and wait
collude and melt away,
leaving me
to the up-wood chill
of the chalk-bone spring
and its downfall.

On an Evening Gently Falling

I have come to a halt where silent rain
drips through the beech trees so slowly

that I catch sadness from young leaves,
held lucent and unlanding in the damp air.

Beneath them are bluebells, which ever make me ache,
bluebells, it seems, cannot be shared with anyone.

What I have cannot express, on an evening gently falling,
their profuse blurred beauty, their hymn

of hummed purple and unwalked green.
The beech trees rise out of them

like a dream in an old wood, vanishing opaque
and withersome into the alone,

on an evening gently falling,
like the rain.

Adrift

Beyond the foot of the lane
a man afloat on the sea lough

hauls the lobster pots in and lets them go
over the red side of his boat.

The day is adrift
on its own drowsiness.

I stand in a ring
of obscure and central feelings

facing the altering water.
I won't know a time before or to come

that can bring you closer
in your absence.

All your living shimmers here,
shivers, rises into the leaning trees of late May's green

where an unseen blackbird,
insistent upon something like delight, sings.

His joy-song suffuses sky, lough and gladed lane,
euphotic as high water.

I drift to the top of the lane where the road
would walk to you or from you,

if you were here.

Showerhead

This evening the shower-hose lies
still in meander in the bath.
Its head inclines, it seems to me,
with the formality of madonna intent on child,
bent in adoration, private, selfless, pure;
madonna of compassion, virgin eleusa;
more commonly realised in marble
than faux chrome with lime-scale
finish in my bath.

Strange in these troubled times
how frequent sightings of the holy family are:
Jesus in a pizza or a piece of ham;
his face in a tree-trunk outside Lidl today
will make News at Ten. Go on, Google it quick.
Click here for more. Perhaps I could vlog
my real-life encounter, make my bathroom
a place of cyber-pilgrimage, a holy
Skype-site for the faithful.

I will not. Instead I will try
to know this tableau of the ordinary:
acrylic bath with plug,
chain draped about the taps,
meandering hose, shampoo
with open lid, a towel
of many pinks and my pyjamas
in an exhausted heap
upon the mat.

Recovery

for my mother

In sunlight she sits
upon the high grass
near a tree which I will soon discover
to be a mulberry.

She watches the south door
of the small stone church
as the guests arrive for a summer
coupling.

I love a weddin' she says
to neither Dad nor me.
We stand separate, deferential,
in the green shade.

I circle a gnarled
trunk, search the cool
undersides of its heart-spun leaves
for early fruit.

In dreamy heat
the minister stares
down the road. The groomsmen
shuffle.

I keep seeing her,
waiting in the sunlight,
wondering what it means to her to witness
the spectacle

of an unknown bride's
arrival to be ringed
at a small world's centre
on a summer's day.

What does she feel?
What strange shyness stops me
from asking, *would* stop me from asking,
if she were here?

Mother Thekla's Question

Something set me searching the other night
for words I'd written in a notebook
years ago,
a holy woman's words,
spoken at a time of crisis for Tavener.

Flicking through the pages
I am surprised to find
in light-blue ink
a self at ease with life, but in black ink
how intense the entries seem

— it comes to me:
the composer
tells Mother Thekla he's depressed
and she replies,
Why should you not be?

Her question shocks my brain
because all the folly of the mind
is seen for what it is: too much
absorption, expectation, too much denial
of the way things merely are.

How hard it is to get beyond the mind
and harder still to stay there,
to keep the sense of where you've been
or to describe it, the way you might a tree,
a loved face or the waves upon the rocks at Malin.

Such as is Borne by a Traveller

Here we are at the Royal Opera House
with our little suitcases on wheels (security-checked)

and a table in the expansive foyer now open to the public
for small coffees and select delicacies served in a refurbed,

particularising space that welcomes inclusivity.
I've been to the gilded Ladies. You're there now,

so I'm alone for a few minutes, with our coats
slung over the spare chairs, suitcases circled like wagons,

as those at the neighbouring tables work in groups
at intense, quasi-spiritual activities.

They're energetic, proactive, ideologically aligned,
all criticism cloaked: *Don't get me wrong…*

I like to sit among these people, the way I might sit
upon a hacksaw, enjoying a thin slice of pain.

I'm outfaced by the urban young, by tapered mothers
who funnel inadequacy to the bulge of my belly, a pang

of something not achieved, something that wouldn't
join or couldn't – or couldn't mend enough to reach.

I appreciate the chance to disburden here today.
Yesterday, I pulled up three snowdrops,

hid them guiltily in my coat, brought them home,
placed them in a transparent vase, watched the bulbs

sink, settle in their held soil, impelling little, green
stems through the aperture towards bent, white heads.

Talking to Each Other

You reach up in the early dawn
to open the window above our bed.
Your bowed belly is warm to my drawn hand,
the night's heat still in you: I imagine journeys,
conjure the sultana and her lover
attuned to birdsong under a cypress tree
in a garden teeming with jasmine, lily, rose,
profuse with pomegranates, figs, plump strawberries
picked from plants that sent out runners, set down
roots, grew out of the wild woods into gardens,
escaped again, climbed into masons' minds,
crept along margins of manuscripts, onto
the corners of handkerchiefs, when you say,
Listen, the doves are talking to each other.

Veduta

I'm making coffee when you bring the paper
and an unexpected ice-cream. I suggest
affogato, ask if you remember walking
between the columns of San Marco and
Teodoro towards the Giardini Biennale,
stopping at an *osteria* on an ordinary street,
one end of which opened onto the lagoon:
a perfect sky over sea that I have measured
blue by, until this spring, when we have lived
at the pace of peonies coming into flower,
watched the coomb green up tree by tree,
entertained by sparrow comedies, kestrel flights
against the vast un-trafficked smoothness of a sky
springing Venetian blue from memory to here.

Delay

Did you spot those cables
at the side of the tunnel entrance
when we were on that train near Ealing?

They were carefully layered, the way
my mother might have laid laundered sheets
in the hot-press. I meant to say.

Inside those grimy cables lies the charge
of the closed circuit, a healthy mix of protons
creating electricity so effectively

that humans have extended days,
subdued the night, domesticated it,
so that with the flick of a switch

or mere verbal command
the world lights up, powers on,
energises everything: laptops, phones,

the oven with our imminent meal,
the robotic lawnmower we saw heady
as a deranged puppy at Montacute on Monday,

even your delayed train, eventually.
I don't know why I wish I'd said something
about the assemblage of dirty cables that day

or at least expressed my short-lived awe
at the conclave of engineers crouched down
over the millions of wires in a box.

I remember thinking of my grandmother,
her life from candles and gaslight
to a bright world I too often take for granted.

As you know, there are days when I prefer the dark,
to see the stars and search out the moon's dust.
Just now I'm imagining our little signals

encased in myelinated sheaths, laid down
along myriad tunnels in ourselves,
tiny charges

leaping across synapses,
firing in marvellous chemical exchange
towards each other.

Bonnard's Bathers at the Tate

Here I am and it is happening already, the
slats of the garden-table and stripes
of your cotton top are mingling
with Marthe's easy pose,
elbow on knee, heel of
her hand on the right
side of her face, sunlight
playing off her chest
and the involuntary
when we turn to each
other. You are still looking
at me, when I look back
at the painting, painted
to regain the past. I step
back for a moment, as
a flash on the water
becomes a woman
with light outlining
her shape, the black
line re-made with
light and you say:
This is like you this
morning, your breasts,
when you sat with
your art magazine
this morning, looking
at the glossy, full-page
image of a colourful
garden.
If you asked me
where I am now, I'd say
beyond the ferry house,
the bridge and the walls
singing with light. I'd
say I'm following your
footsteps through people,
and a path winding
between your breasts,
life before is coming
and going, life now

resumes, as you look
at a painting you kept
as a postcard for years,
while I re-imagine
the bathers' print on
my wall, how I love
bathing, its optimism.
You believe Marthe
is hurting more
than I do – but I
could be wrong.
A photographer
moves in to capture
the bather so up close
that we can see her
fragments caught
in the viewfinder.
When we are not drawn
to this, still we stand
drawn to each other.
The limes shimmer
in the full foliage of
a warm day and the
house among them
arrives. Always the
project is summer,
warmth, timelessness
of time together. You
say this painting of
Marthe is like a photo
you took of yourself.
I look at you realise
your devastation,
understand
I have forgotten
mine.

Tessellations

A chilly gust of wind blows through your ribs and is decomposing you.
You no longer have an ear. Your neck has vanished.

                                                            Franca Mancinelli

You talk about a virtual event giving an Italian poet
a platform to reach an audience beyond her own language.
You recall her *poesie scelte*, its rhythms.
I want to tell you, but your mind is full
as you serve out *spaghetti arrabbiata* and talk
about emotion in a language you don't understand.
I am trying to stay with you but am thinking
of my search for Frampton online and where
we walked on Sunday past the shrunken
village down the sloping field to the absence
on the flint platform under the overgrowth,
where I spread my arms and tried to conjure
a villa or a Roman temple through which
the ritual of water might have run.

You are talking about the importance of translation
but I want to tell you I have found illustrations
of the lost mosaics from the building we could not see;
one pavement contained a poem inscribed in Latin
in catalectic anapaestic dimeters that no one can translate
for sure, nor is it certain what all the figures mean:
are Bacchus, Neptune, Cupid with dolphins
linked to the *chi rho* in the apse or the mythic lovers
in the corners or the damaged hunters on horseback?
The makers of these mosaics are not known, nor
are those who laid them, lost them, found them,
drew or defaced them, re-buried what was left.
We keep setting down in words and other means
our myths, our acts of love – we keep repeating.

First Outing in Months to a Hillside with Cliff Edge

We have made a conscious effort to embrace
the action as if it is really happening,
but for now, my love, let's sit here side by side,
you, reading the map, and I'll lie back imagining
the audience at Milos, seated on the tiered hillside
overlooking the sea, gaze fixed on the masked actors,
goat-blood running red as sorrel down the slope,
while offstage deaths accumulate, voices warn
that the theatres are too full or too empty,
so buskin, satyr, sock remain the stock choices.
Daily rituals of grief and laughter play out
in our fridge-door dramas, in the shared shadows
of zoomed distance, in the round of our own skulls,
as we await our fate in the next utterance.

Diogenes got up and walked

Both leaden and argentine is the surface
of the lake and *grow* says the grass

down the middle of the road.
The church stones crumble.

A pair of dog-walkers
with one voice say *happy*,

then *lonely*, but what they say in between
blows away on the breeze.

I go climbing
the natural sleeve of the lane

out into head-talk of birds and swirling
leaves. The ditch

smells
like a sack of the dead.

One loose hen picks at the possibilities
in this heaving habitat of wither.

Sudden pings from my pocket
offer little circles of affirmation,

but images of *palazzi* and distant greetings
disturb, so I return

the phone to my pocket and my gaze
to the road

where the gape of a headless squirrel
hardens

on the grassy trivet of the lane.

Presentiments

You can see it from here: that man in the Merc
is on the verge of a crash. He's edgy
in the standing traffic, nervy.
I want to say: *You're not safe,*
imagine his realisation, acknowledgement,
instead, he revs off – brakes – revs off –

I stare into the up-close coats of passers-by,
think about this friend of yours, the anger
in her face when I said: *This is no time to talk.*
She looked at me with hard eyes, said:
You know what you can do with your truisms.
I replied: *They're all I have.*

For a moment it silenced her and I thought
we'd leave, but you stood on; ironic
that saying *no time to talk*
made it possible for you to do just that.
Let's go, I whispered to myself,
returned to the car, where I wait...

*

I remember when I lived alone,
accepted a loose invitation to a party,
given by a sturdy American
in a fiercely book-lined apartment,
with a colour scheme I'd call 'combative'.
It took only one glass of the red
and *amuse bouche*
to know I should slip away...

I remember standing next to a tall, literary lady
in a first-floor drawing room
that gave onto a sloping, tree-lined avenue.
She said: *There's my Persephone coming to me now.*
I watched an older woman make her slow way
up the hill. I saw her sway, knew
she would collapse, heard the stricken cry:
My Persephone!

Mixed Signals

Why does the red of a rose not mean *stop*?
Why does the red of a traffic-light not mean *love*?

Signals misfire – the system overworked,
understaffed, at breaking-point,

trying to manage the confusion,
such as the kiss, or was it loss, we shared last night,

the curl of your arm about my waist,
the way you left.

These words are not what it was, my love.
This poem is not what it is.

Waiting for the Departure Gate to be Announced at Belfast City Airport

Lemons and silver were on the windowsill
when you told me yesterday about the Spartans,
not that we know of them directly,
they have no literature of their own, you said,
but from others' writings we have learned
something of them, how they lived. Why
from all the moments we shared yesterday
do I remember this? There was something
I wanted to say at the time but couldn't,
something I wanted to understand about you,
about me, about the bleak world I need
to see as beautiful as the lemons and silver
on your windowsill, their zest and gleam.

A man whistles *Here comes the sun,*
stares out over the wet runway, the dismal
hangars and hills hidden in morning mist.
Burly laughter erupts at a breakfast-table,
thick with fries. I suffer sympathetic indigestion,
play Wordle (envoy, lemon, stone), trail
round the bookshop, full of *Difficult
Births*, *Unsettled People*. The front-pages
declare: *Stalemate in Stormont*, *Death
of Former Pope*. All manner of stories
leave me on the wrong side of things,
with the perennial, partisan fear
of being wrong. What strange bone
in my body imagines allegiance
to a cause, resistance even,
just as quickly sloughs it off –
Gate 7
Responses ripple, become purposeful.
I hold back from competition to the gate.
All I can think of is a silver urn
holding nine hundred gallons of Ganges
water for a travelling maharajah
and the half lemon on your windowsill.

States of Matter

I must not go looking
for a saviour or
a swaddling group.
I must not imagine
that the salient
aspects of my suffering
can be shared. I must
not imagine that my worth
hangs on those aspects
of myself of which
others might approve.
It might seem easier
to deposit my distress,
the minute particulars
of my own fears, with
others, but the nature
of suffering is individual
and served inadequately
by groups. I'm better
moving toward comfort
with my own discomfort.
I'll start in the body,
name each precise
discord. I'll lean in
and live with them.
I'll keep breathing,
if that doesn't sound
absurd, and in the odd
alchemy of observance
and breath, I'll forsake
old pathways, think
along new ones, become
most of the help I will
ever need, not forgetting
that all thoughts condense
to attitude and, without
care, can harden into creed.
What to do but understand
the changing state of matter,
remember that bricks
are made of clay,

and clay of dust;
that rocks
have other states:
melting to liquid,
they sublimate
to gas.

Seaside, Seesaws and Other Oscillations

I'm so serious I signed up for a laughter course,
that went well until I cried,

so I quit in week four, believing I'd wrung out
sufficient tissues, actually grasping by week three

that the place for me was at the pivot
of a seesaw, one foot either side of the fulcrum,

moving slightly up or slightly down,
adapting to load.

Days began to look different, nights too,
because I'd found a way to think, an image,

then another popped in – of Weymouth
in the winter and me

walking backwards along the prom – it turns out
that walking backwards along the prom

is good for me – the Chinese say a hundred steps back
are worth a thousand steps forward – and I see

that relentless forward motion has taken me
nowhere. I do love Weymouth in the winter,

where a man from his mobility scooter warns
the rail-replacement bus has broken down,

an ambulance goes by, strapped
to a recovery vehicle, blue lights blazing –

and there's a seagull with a limp. Oh, the brokenness,
the difficulties pile up, but I can bear it.

When the entrance to the nearby shop
says *Please use other door*

and the other door says *We're closed,*
I can stand on my seesaw and laugh.

I can grin like a collapsed jack o'lantern
outside a second home. I do love Weymouth

in the winter. The busker sings: *We'll take
our clothes off and go dancing...*

Old King George must be cold on his plinth
but he bears it. I have my seesaw,

I have Weymouth in the winter
and walking backwards along the prom,

where last week I saw a woman stranded on the beach.
A man held her, but couldn't heave her up.

They locked elbows, rocked back and forth,
until by a miracle of combined forces, she rose to her feet,

to warm whoops, loud laughter and bundling hugs
that stayed with me,

as a December chill rose off the wide bay
and the day dropped

into the lazy, dusky, navy sea,
with the moon rising.

Positive Silence After Poetry

And what do I think now
after the event – everyone
I meet is smiling, making
eye contact, nodding hello
and I'm thinking it must
be Saturday in their faces
until it strikes that I'm
the smiler and what
I'm giving out
I'm getting back.
Who knew positivity
could be this simple?
Well, I did, but must
learn it over and over
and o this river
is wise, the walk
across it is so deep,
everything is a journey
of thought and what I
am able to get down is
only the dance troupe
literally skipping across
the bridge, the absolute
regiment of mini cyclists,
the Nobel peace prize in
the Guildhall, colouration
in Bartlett's last map,
a diversity crossing,
coffee in Foyleside
under the escalator,
fearful that something
might fall on my head,
but it's the chocolate
egg on my cornflake
bun, that just as I'm
about to bite that
falls, so I am agape,
a mouth – that was
one of Willie's gentle
insults, *Ya mouth ye*,

though he never
insulted me. *Poetry's
a mouth,* says Auden
and a bare-armed
woman chatters
on this cold day –
I get this down
– this is all
I get down,
when there's so
much more arriving
with the people,
so many thoughts
running behind
their faces, under
their talking, if only
I got more down,
or perhaps what
I need is silence.
I wish I was more
able for it or for
more of it, better
able to manage
without words.
After the reading
a woman said,
*Your pauses
were amazing,*
so perhaps I'm
already on the
road to silence,
its perfection,
though to
paraphrase
Saint Augustine
I do hope to
get there
but not
quite
yet.

On Going a Journey

Gather beneath the first letter
of the alphabet and begin.
Grow with the community,
learning to count each spoke
in the wheel. Begin to walk,
then travel, passing through
twelve spring-bolt gates,
staying in single file, till you
reach the top. Once there,
listen to the unspoken and
wait for new moons to arrive.
Know love, gentle as breath
on a naked leaf, fierce
as gales on howling trunks.
Hold fast, till all chlorophyll
has ebbed away and learn to die
again and again, un-medalled,
wearing grace in the button-hole
of your heart. Husband the lonely
thoughts and weave the empty
sunshine through the lanes
to form a pattern out of wild
life. Peer down the natural
nave, beyond the green panel
on the western door, to seek
but never find the artist. Desist
from watching the shadow
of your own hand but dream
on, beaming, like beryllium
synthesised in stars. Scatter
laughter freely as you go.
If foot-sore, sling a hammock
between ash and oak, rest
and reflect the distant choices.
When ready, set out alone
for the long-handled gate.
Proceed upwards, still
breathing Shakespeare,
until you pass from human
sight but do not leave.

Lough Shore Nocturne

Dusk brings the island closer,
the gone hours held in deepening fields.

Perspective is liquid, an ever-turning
mystery of tides.

Night blooms along the shoreline,
dissolving form,

all difference fades to shared
dark.

Light exists only in points,
the island hillside

a landed constellation,
its own plough – and I wish

you were here beside me,
as day succumbs and night invites,

but you are another place,
a vanished island staring back at me,

seeing your own starships in my shape,
feeling your own loss,

wishing for me a little, knowing
I do not soothe.

The sea-lough between us
is unbridgeable,

its currents deceptive, all crossings
inadvisable,

the once familiar shore
beyond reach.

On the Morning of my Sixtieth Birthday

I have the wide view to myself,
this swathe of sea lough, its tidal
force, pushing water towards
the shore on this overcast day
in April, the high horizon
not saw-teeth, but a swag
of worn molars, the blunted
wisdom of blue mountains,
but what I still have is breath,
exhalation, the dare-I-say-it
happiness of here, a history
in the low hills, in myself,
on this furrowed foreshore,
where ripples frill the brown
rocks and seaweed is shaggy
over them – it is both now
and the possibility of future
with light ever shifting on
the surface, that is gathering.
Take it by the throat, was
what the man said yesterday.
I suppressed a gulp, thinking
his metaphor was not for me,
but his meaning was: I fear
going deep and, indeed, am
fearful of the lurking, unseen
slippery; of buried nips; teeth;
fins; tentacles; stings; even
of creatures that don't exist,
I fear the possibility. He says
to push on but nearby signage
says *Watch out for unprotected edge.*
I see the scatter of rocks, salt
water rushing over and round,
I see my limits for grasping
the flung moment, know of
unseen forces shifting below
and on the surface. I don't
wish for the end of currents,
only to evade the treacherous.
I want airiness, clarity, to be
a speck on the beach,

to be one, to be a multiple
of insignificance, worked
by water, blown by wind,
hurled through days when
there is nothing to hold onto,
once I've let go.

Notes

City Café, 1968: The conflict in Northern Ireland known as the Troubles arguably started on October 5th 1968, when violence erupted between the security forces and protesters on a Northern Ireland Civil Rights Association march in Derry/Londonderry. I was at a wedding reception in the City Café, Shipquay Street, close to the location of the violence. I was four years old.

Gap: By the end of 1971, 29 barricades were in place in the city to block access to what was called 'Free Derry'. Cars and other vehicles were hijacked to build the barricades.

Great-aunt Maggie: The 'no go' areas maintained by factions of the IRA were designed to keep police and British troops out of those areas. The City Cemetery lay inside this 'no go' area, as did the homes of some Protestant families, including my great-aunt Maggie's.

Bloody Monday references 'Bloody Sunday', the name given to the murders in Derry/Londonderry, Northern Ireland on Sunday, January 30th 1972 by British paratroopers at a Civil Rights demonstration in which 13, later 14, people were killed.

A New Cousin: In the weeks and months after 'Bloody Sunday', the IRA and other paramilitaries intensified their campaigns of violence.

Next-door Neighbours: The explosion in Ferryquay Street referred to occurred at 4.25pm on Wednesday, 1st March 1972.

Claudy: On 31st July the British Government implemented Operation Motorman which aimed to remove all 'no go' areas in Northern Ireland. Four people were killed. On the same day the IRA detonated three car bombs in the village of Claudy, eleven miles from Derry / Londonderry, killing 9 people including Kathryn Eakin, an 8 year old girl.

Afloat: This poem sprang from seeing a painting on display at Torre Abbey in Devon. It was by Dorothea Sharp (1873-1955), a landscape artist who specialised in studies of children at play, often on beaches. I now refer to any poem about playing on beaches as 'a Dorothea'.

Isolated Shooting Incident: 'Red Caps' was a nickname for Military Policemen or MPs, whose role was to police army service personnel. They patrolled unarmed on occasions such as the one described here. Within a few hours of the incident recalled in *Isolated Shooting Incident*, a brief report was published in the north-west edition of the *Belfast Telegraph*. This is part of it: '*Shots were fired at a two man Military Police patrol. Two youths and two teenage girls were carrying an Armalite rifle and a pistol…A nine year old child who had earlier been talking to the MPs was only a few feet in front when the attack took place.*' I was quite upset that my age was wrongly reported. I was eight, not nine. My mother kept the newspaper snippet. I came upon it, after her death in 2014.

The Price of Violence: This poem is about the filming and broadcasting of a BBC documentary investigating the impact of violence on children in Northern Ireland in 1972. It was presented by Harold Williamson and exists in the BBC archives: *Tuesday Documentary: The Price of Violence, 14ᵗʰ November 1972 (BBC1 9.25p.m.).*

The Price of Violence: 'shiny 50p piece'. On Monday 15ᵗʰ February 1971 decimalisation had taken place in the UK and Ireland.

Endeavour / Routine Tuesday at the Girls' Brigade: My family attended regular organisations at our local Presbyterian church in Carlisle Road. Christian Endeavour was on Monday, Girls' Brigade on Tuesday, Boys' Brigade on Thursday, choir practice on Friday. On Sunday there were two church services at 11.30am and 6.00pm, with Sunday School for children in Carlisle Road at 10.30am. My brother and I attended a further Sunday School in Lower Bennett Street at 3.00pm.

Coleraine: In Coleraine, Northern Ireland on Tuesday 12ᵗʰ June 1973 the Provisional IRA detonated two car bombs, killing 6 pensioners and injuring 33 people (a number of them school children).

Learning to Swim: The Rossville Flats in the Bogside were the first high rise flats to be built outside Belfast. 'Free Derry' was the name given to the area of the Bogside that the RUC and British Army did not enter between 1969 and 1972. 'Free Derry' wall (a gable wall of a row of terraced houses) became a key meeting point for rallies in the Bogside.

Sharp Shooter: I was not allowed to play for the school's football team, despite 'running rings' round many of the boys who did play (according to Derek Lyttle). However, the following year the rules were changed but I had moved on to secondary school and taken up hockey instead.

A Dance Lesson: The song I heard at that dance lesson is called *'Soldier'* by Harvey Andrews. I remembered fragments of this song for over half a century and tracked it down when writing this poem. The song was inspired by the self-sacrifice of Sergeant Michael Willetts. The song was written and recorded in 1972, then released as the B-side of the single (or 45) *In the Darkness*. It was subsequently banned for a time by the BBC, as Andrews' intention not to take sides in the conflict was misunderstood.

Cul-de-sac: I was born in a cul-de-sac of terraced houses lived in by working class Protestants and Catholics. Cook Terrace is one side of the street. Mary Street is the other. Protestants and Catholics lived on both sides. Protestants no longer live there.

Scene Around Six was the title of the BBC Regional News programme in the Seventies.

Why We Leave Cook Terrace references the movement of Protestants from the west bank of the city due to intimidation and fear. It is a matter of fact that the Protestant population of the West Bank of Derry/Londonderry decreased by 66% between '71 and '81 – and has continued to decline. Only one Protestant working class area remains on the cityside. It has a population of around 300 residents.

Grinning Bobby: Robert (Bobby) Stott, 22, shirt-cutter and part-time member of the UDR was shot dead near his home in the Fountain on 25th November 1975. The killing was condemned by all sides of the community in Derry/Londonderry.

Fifty Years On: See note on *Coleraine*.

Keep Walking: This poem refers back to the events in *Cul-de-sac*.

Privilege: More than 3500 people were killed in The Troubles. More than half of these victims were civilians without links to the security forces or to paramilitary groups. The city's previously integrated working class communities were destroyed.

The Road to Shroove: The van which says *Make Me Up* belongs to a local beautician whose services are available for formals, wedding parties, hen parties etc.

They Came Out of the Mist: An overview of Ireland from the first hunter-gatherers to the present day.

Votive: Manannan Mac Lir (the son of the Sea) is the most significant sea deity of Irish mythology. According to local folklore, he is said to be buried off the coast of Inishowen. Treasure from the 1st century B.C. called the Broighter Hoard which includes a stunning tiny golden boat, complete with oars, is thought to be a votive offering to Mac Lir.

Three Pints along the Inishowen 100: The *Inis Eoghain* 100 is a scenic route around the Inishowen peninsula of County Donegal, Ireland. Locations mentioned in the poems include Wee White Strand, Port-na-garley, Tremone, Dungree Point, Shroove, Greencastle, Moville and Malin.

A Wide River Divides Us offers a perspective on Derry/Londonderry approximately fifty years after the events of my childhood. Many improvements have been made to the city, but the continuing political impasse, exacerbated by the destabilising effects of Brexit and other events, leaves the future less secure than it has appeared in recent years.

Palmer's Moon: Samuel Palmer (1805-1881) was an English landscape painter, central to a mystical group of painters called The Ancients, who were inspired by William Blake. My poem also references W.B. Yeats's *Lines Written in Dejection* (1920).

Any developed south-easterly or easterly condition, or a southerly gale, will cause the sea to break so heavily at the entrance as to make the harbour unapproachable: This lengthy title comes from a weather report by *eoceanic* regarding conditions in West Bay Harbour, Dorset in 2018.

Mother Thekla's Question: The composer John Tavener spoke on BBC Radio 4's *Desert Island Discs* on Sunday, 18th September 1994 about the importance of Mother Thekla in his life. Mother Thekla was a teacher, a nun and founder of the Orthodox Monastery of the Assumption in North Yorkshire.

Veduta: Italian term for a painting of a view or a vista.

Bonnard's Bather at the Tate refers to the French painter Pierre Bonnard who frequently painted his wife and muse, Marthe, in the act of bathing. The exhibition at the Tate in 2018 was called 'The Colour of Memory'.

Tessellations: The original Italian reads: 'Un soffio di freddo ti attraversa le costole e tis ta scomponendo. Non hai piu un orecchio. Il tuo collo e svanito.' It comes from Franca Mancinelli's *Libretto di Transito / The Little Book of Passage*, translated from the Italian by John Taylor (The Bitter Oleander Press, 2018) and was also published in *Before Words Become Hot Wax: Selected Poems* by Franca Mancinelli, translated by John Taylor (Versopolis Four, Ledbury Poetry Festival, 2020).

First Outing in Months to a Hillside with Cliff Edge: The poem references Greek drama. The terms 'buskin' and 'sock' refer to the actors' footwear for tragedy and comedy.

Seaside, Seesaws and Other Oscillations: the idea of walking backwards for health purposes arose from the late Dr Michael Mosley's BBC Radio 4 Series: *Just One Thing*, which aired on 15 November 2023.

Positive Silence After Poetry: The church on the oldest ecclesiastical site in Derry/Londonderry is that of St Augustine. To this saint is attributed the prayer that God should make him chaste – but not yet!

Acknowledgements

I would like to thank the editors of *The New Humanist, Bad Lilies, The Honest Ulsterman, Trasna, Atrium, erbacce press, Harvest* and *Matter out of Place*, who included my poems, or earlier versions of them, in their publications.

The epigraph to *Tessellations* is used by kind permission of Franca Mancinelli.

Thanks to Patryk Sadowki for the cover image.

Warm thanks to the following for their advice, encouragement and confidence in my work: Greta Stoddart, Fiona Sampson, Elaine Beckett, Helen Evans, Annie Freud, Pam Zinnemann-Hope, Cathie Hartigan, James Kerr, Jonathan Burgess and Cinnamon Press. My thanks to the numerous poets and writers with whom I have engaged in person and online over many years, in a rich and generous exchange of ideas.

Lastly, heartfelt thanks to dear friends and family, especially to my father, for his humour and steady good sense.

I gratefully acknowledge the support of the Northern Ireland Arts Council.